I Care About...
MY PLANET

Liz Lennon

W
FRANKLIN WATTS
LONDON • SYDNEY

Franklin Watts

First published in Great Britain in 2020 by The Watts Publishing Group
Copyright © The Watts Publishing Group, 2020

ISBN (HB): 978 1 4451 7191 3
ISBN (PB): 978 1 4451 7192 0

Printed in Dubai

Series Editor: Sarah Peutrill
Design: Collaborate
Illustration: Michael Buxton

Franklin Watts
An imprint of
Hachette Children's Group
Part of The Watts Publishing Group
Carmelite House
50 Victoria Embankment
London EC4Y 0DZ
An Hachette UK Company

www.hachette.co.uk
www.franklinwatts.co.uk

FSC
www.fsc.org

MIX
Paper from
responsible sources
FSC® C104740

Contents

Earth is amazing

You and more than seven billion other people live on planet Earth. The planet is our home. It gives us everything we need – water, food, shelter and air to breathe.

Planet Earth has to be cared for. We shouldn't waste things like water that the Earth provides. If we don't look after Earth, it can't look after us.

Watery planet

When you look at a picture of the Earth, most of it looks blue. That's because Earth is covered in oceans of water. All animals and plants need water to live but most of the water on the planet is salty sea water. We need to take care not to waste water.

What can I do?

- You can take showers instead of baths.
- In the garden use the water butt to water the plants.
- Paddling pools use a lot of water – why not play with squeezy bottles in the garden instead.

Litter

Litter is the things we don't want that ends up on the ground, in ponds, lakes and the sea. It could be plastic bottles, crisp packets or sweet wrappers. Litter can hurt wildlife. Put your litter in a bin or take it home if there isn't one.

9

Turn off the lights

Energy is used to power things like the lights and the machines in your home. Most of this energy comes from power stations. Some power stations use fuel such as coal or oil. These are taken from the ground and will one day run out. It's important not to waste energy.

What can I do?

Here are some ways your family can save energy at home. Think of some ways you can help.

• Only put the washing machine on when it is full.

• Dry the clothes outside, not in a dryer.

• Turn off the lights when you leave a room.

Get walking

Cars are a useful way to get around but they also need energy to move. Most cars are powered using petrol. That's another of the Earth's resources that will run out one day. Cars also cause pollution – they make the air dirty.

What can I do?

- If you are going on a short journey, it's best to walk, cycle or scoot.

- If you are going further, can you take a bus or train?

Wonderful trees

Trees are important. They are the biggest plants on Earth. They give us oxygen, which is part of the air we breathe. They are a home for wildlife. They give us food and materials for tools and shelter. Trees are also beautiful to look at.

Food

Medicines

Trees give ...

Paper

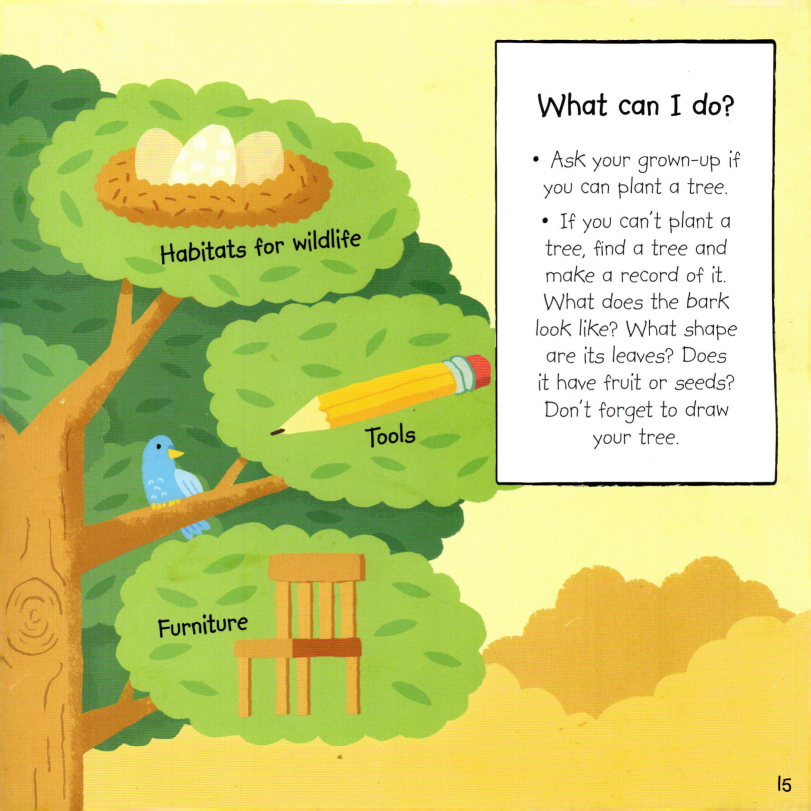

Habitats for wildlife

Tools

Furniture

What can I do?

• Ask your grown-up if you can plant a tree.

• If you can't plant a tree, find a tree and make a record of it. What does the bark look like? What shape are its leaves? Does it have fruit or seeds? Don't forget to draw your tree.

Paper

Do you love drawing on fresh paper?
Paper is brilliant stuff, but do you know where
it comes from? Trees are grown and chopped
down to make paper – so don't waste it!

What can I do?

Here's some ways to save paper:

- Reuse envelopes
- Draw on both sides of a piece of paper
- Use old birthday and Christmas cards to make gift tags.

What other ways can you think of to save paper?

Reduce waste

All the materials we use to make things come from the Earth. One of the best ways to help the planet is not to waste things. When we buy new things they are made and packaged in materials.

What can I do?

Is your room full of toys? Think how you can reduce waste. For example:

- Ask yourself if you need new toys – can you make one instead, perhaps?
- Swap toys with friends.
- Look in charity shops for toys that other people no longer want.

Food waste

We use a lot of the planet to grow
the food that we and farm animals eat.
When the crops have grown, it is put
in packaging and taken to shops.
It's important not to waste your food.

What can I do?

- Don't put more on your plate than you can eat.

- Don't turn down fruit and vegetables that have little marks on or are a bit wonky. They will still be tasty!

Where rubbish goes

So what happens to your rubbish? Some things can be recycled and made into new things. Not everything gets recycled though. A lot of rubbish is buried under the ground. Places to bury rubbish will one day run out.

What can I do?

These things can be recycled – so don't put them in the rubbish bin.
(Check with your grown-up):

- paper
- some plastics
- aluminium cans
- food can be recycled into compost.

Plastic

You may have heard people talking about plastic being bad. Plastic is not all bad. It is a very useful material that can be made into all sorts of things. The trouble is that plastic does not break down and disappear quickly when it is buried. It can take hundreds of years.

Plastic rubbish also gets into the rivers and oceans where it is eaten by fish and other animals. Try not to waste plastic. Use a reusable water bottle. Don't use a plastic bag once and throw it away.

Plants and animals

All the plants and animals around you should be cared for. Plants feed insects and other animals. In turn insects do important jobs like helping plants to grow, and being food for birds and other animals. All of nature is linked together.

What can I do?

Here are some ways you can care for nature in your area:

- If you have a garden you could ask your grown-up if you can set up a bird feeder.

- Don't hurt minibeasts like worms, snails and bees – be careful where you tread!

- Learn all you can about animals.

Enjoy your world

The Earth is an amazing place. Get to know this special home. When you're out, look for plants, trees and animals. Learn the name of each type. Don't forget to take your litter home!

What can I do?

Here are some things you could do with your grown-up:

- Go for a paddle in a stream.
- Collect leaves from the ground and make a picture.
- Grow some flowers or vegetables from seeds.

What else can you think of to do to enjoy your world?

Remember

Don't waste paper, plastic, food or water.

Litter goes in the bin.

Save the energy in your home by switching off lights.

Walking is better for the planet than using a car.

Take care of the nature around you.

Reuse if you can, rather than buying new things.

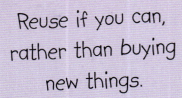

Enjoy your world.

Useful words

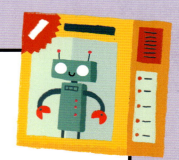

Oxygen   an invisible gas in the air that we breathe in

Packaging   materials that are used to surround something we buy, such as a new toy

Power station   a place where electricity is produced

Recycling   turning something we've used into something new

Shelter   a place that shields us from the weather

Index